Cambridge English

Movers 9

Answer Booklet

Cambridge University Press
www.cambridge.org/elt

Cambridge English Language Assessment
www.cambridgeenglish.org

Information on this title: www.cambridge.org/9781107464247

© Cambridge University Press and UCLES 2015

First published 2015
Reprinted 2016

Printed in Italy by Rotolito Lombarda S.p.A.

A catalogue record for this publication is available from the British Library

ISBN 978-1-107-46432-2 Student's Book
ISBN 978-1-107-46424-7 Answer Booklet
ISBN 978-1-107-46426-1 Audio CD

Contents

Introduction   4

Test 1 Answers   6

Test 2 Answers   12

Test 3 Answers   18

Combined *Starters* and *Movers*
Thematic Vocabulary List   24

Introduction

The *Cambridge English: Young Learners* tests offer an elementary-level testing system (up to CEFR level A2) for learners of English between the ages of 7 and 12. The tests include three key levels of assessment: *Starters*, *Movers* and *Flyers*.

Movers is the second level in the system. Test instructions are very simple and consist only of words and structures specified in the syllabus.

The complete test lasts about an hour and has the following components: Listening, Reading and Writing, and Speaking.

	length	number of parts	number of questions
Listening	approx. 25 minutes	5	25
Reading and Writing	30 minutes	6	40
Speaking	approx. 5–7 minutes	4	–

Candidates need a pen or pencil for the Reading and Writing paper, and coloured pens or pencils for the Listening paper. All answers are written on the question papers.

Listening

In general, the aim is to focus on the 'here and now' and to use language in meaningful contexts. In addition to multiple-choice and short-answer questions, candidates are asked to use coloured pencils to mark their responses to one task. There are five parts. Each part begins with a clear example.

part	main skill focus	input	expected response	number of questions
1	the main skill focus in all five parts of the Listening test is listening for specific information of various kinds, e.g. numbers, describing people etc.	picture, names and dialogue	draw lines to match names to people in a picture	5
2		form or page of notepad with missing words and dialogue	write words or numbers in gaps	5
3		pictures, days of the week and dialogue	draw lines from days of week to correct pictures	5
4		3-option multiple-choice pictures and dialogues	tick box under correct picture	5
5		picture and dialogue	carry out instructions to colour, draw and write (range of colours is: black, blue, brown, green, grey, orange, pink, purple, red, yellow)	5

Reading and Writing

Again, the focus is on the 'here and now' and the use of language in meaningful contexts where possible. To complete the test, candidates need a single pen or pencil of any colour. There are six parts, each starting with a clear example.

part	main skill focus	input	expected response	number of items
1	reading short definitions and matching to words writing words	labelled pictures and definitions	copy the correct words next to the definitions	6
2	reading sentences about a picture and writing one-word answers	one picture and sentences	write 'yes' or 'no'	6
3	reading a dialogue and choosing the correct responses	one picture and short dialogue with multiple-choice responses	choose correct response by circling a letter	6
4	reading for specific information and gist copying words	cloze text, words and pictures	choose and copy missing words correctly; tick a box to choose the best title for the story	7
5	reading a story and completing sentences about the story	story, pictures and gapped sentences	completing sentences about story by writing 1, 2 or 3 words	10
6	reading and understanding a factual text copying words	gapped text and 3-option multiple choice (grammatical words)	complete text by selecting the correct words and copying them in corresponding gaps	5

Speaking

In the Speaking test, the candidate speaks with one examiner for about six minutes. The format of the test is explained in advance to the child in their native language by a teacher or person familiar to them. This person then takes the child into the exam room and introduces them to the examiner.

Speaking ability is assessed according to various criteria, including comprehension, the ability to produce an appropriate response and pronunciation.

part	main skill focus	input	expected response
1	describing two pictures by using short responses	two similar pictures	identify four differences between pictures
2	understanding the beginning of a story and then continuing it based on a series of pictures	picture sequence	describe each picture in turn
3	suggesting a picture which is different and explaining why	picture sets	identify the odd one out and give reason
4	understanding and responding to personal questions	open-ended questions about candidate	answer personal questions

Further information

Further information about *Cambridge English: Young Learners* can be obtained from:

Cambridge English Language Assessment
1 Hills Road
Cambridge CB1 2EU
United Kingdom

www.cambridgeenglish.org/help
www.cambridgeenglish.org/younglearners

Test 1 Answers

Listening

Part 1 (5 marks)

Lines should be drawn between:

1 Sally and the older girl carrying drinks, wearing a blue flower in her hair
2 Peter and the boy sitting on the floor with a board game, looking angry
3 Jane and the girl with long hair, laughing, in front of the TV
4 Jim and the man standing on the balcony, in a red jacket
5 Paul and the man coming into the room, with no shoes on

Part 2 (5 marks)

1 clean   2 bread   3 bus   4 daughter   5 Gill (correct spelling)

Part 3 (5 marks)

1 Wednesday – played football
2 Friday – visited farm, rode on farmer's truck
3 Tuesday – did pictures of sheep and cows
4 Saturday – watched a film
5 Thursday – reading and writing about farms

Part 4 (5 marks)

1 C   2 B   3 C   4 B   5 A

Part 5 (5 marks)

1 Colour the small road with the bike on it – yellow
2 Colour the two leaves on the ground – red
3 Draw a star on the boy's sweater
4 Colour the bigger cloud – blue
5 Colour the flying bird – pink

TRANSCRIPT   *Hello. This is the Cambridge English Movers Listening Test.*

Part 1   *Look at Part 1. Now look at the picture. Listen and look. There is one example.*

[pause]

BOY: I took a photo at my uncle and aunt's flat yesterday. I like going there because I've got a lot of cousins.
WOMAN: Can I see?
BOY: Yes. There's my favourite cousin. She's called Vicky.
WOMAN: The girl on the sofa?
BOY: Yes. You can only see her legs and the top of her head.

[pause]

Can you see the line? This is an example. Now you listen and draw lines.

[pause]

1

WOMAN: Who's that? The girl who's carrying the drinks?
BOY: With the blue flower in her hair?
WOMAN: Yes.
BOY: Oh, that's Sally, but she doesn't like her name.
WOMAN: Why not?
BOY: I don't know.

[pause]

2

BOY: And there's Peter ...
WOMAN: Where?
BOY: He's sitting on the floor.

WOMAN: Why does he look angry?
BOY: Because he's losing the game!

[pause]

3

WOMAN: Are the two girls who are watching TV your cousins too?
BOY: Yes. I've got seven cousins!
WOMAN: Wow!
BOY: The one with the longer hair is Jane. She's laughing. Can you see?
WOMAN: Oh, yes.

[pause]

4

WOMAN: And who's the man who's standing on the balcony?
BOY: In the red jacket? He's my uncle's friend.
WOMAN: And what's his name?
BOY: Ermm … it's Jim, I think. Yes, that's right.

[pause]

5

WOMAN: And who's that?
BOY: The man who's coming in the room?
WOMAN: Yes. Is that your uncle?
BOY: Yes! My uncle Paul. He's great.
WOMAN: Why isn't he wearing shoes?
BOY: Because they were wet, I think.

[pause]

Now listen to Part 1 again.

[The recording is repeated.]

That is the end of Part 1.

[pause]

Part 2 *Listen and look. There is one example.*

[pause]

GIRL: Excuse me. Can I ask you some questions about shopping in this supermarket?
MAN: All right …
GIRL: It's for my homework. I have to write about shopping.
MAN: Oh, OK.
GIRL: Do you come shopping in the morning or in the afternoon?
MAN: In the morning.

[pause]

Can you see the answer? Now you listen and write.

[pause]

1

GIRL: Why do you like this supermarket?
MAN: I like it because it's always clean …
GIRL: Clean?

MAN: Yes, you can see that.
GIRL: OK. Thank you.

[pause]

2

GIRL: And is there something that you buy here every day?
MAN: Ermm …
GIRL: Do you always buy milk?
MAN: No, but I always buy bread.
GIRL: Bread … OK, thanks.

[pause]

3

GIRL: Now, one more question … Do you come here in a car?
MAN: I have got a car, but I come here on the bus because it's easier.
GIRL: You carry all your shopping on the bus? That's difficult.
MAN: No! Not for me.

[pause]

4

GIRL: And do you do all the shopping in your family?
MAN: Oh no, my daughter helps me.
GIRL: Ah! Is your daughter here now?
MAN: Yes, she's looking for some coffee that we saw on TV.

[pause]

5

GIRL: Now can you tell me your name, please?
MAN: Yes, it's Mr Gill.
GIRL: Can you spell that for me please, Mr Gill?
MAN: Yes. It's G-I-double L.
GIRL: Thanks a lot. Bye.

[pause]

Now listen to Part 2 again.

[The recording is repeated.]

That is the end of Part 2.

[pause]

Part 3 *Look at the pictures. What did Jack do last week? Listen and look. There is one example.*

[pause]

WOMAN: What did you do at school last week, Jack?
BOY: Oh … lots of things. On Monday, a man came to talk to my class.
WOMAN: Did he? What about?
BOY: About his work. He's a farmer. He's got lots of sheep.
WOMAN: Did he bring one with him?
BOY: No!

[pause]

Can you see the line from the word Monday? On Monday, a man came to the school to talk to Jack's class. Now you listen and draw lines.

[pause]

1

BOY: We had a good game of football one afternoon.
WOMAN: At school?
BOY: Yes. There's a field behind the school. It's part of the farm, but we can play there.
WOMAN: That's good. Which afternoon was that?
BOY: It was on Wednesday, I think. Yes, that's right.

[pause]

2

WOMAN: And what about Friday?
BOY: Ermm ... we worked all day in the classroom, I think ... No, that's wrong. After lunch, the teacher took us out.
WOMAN: Why?
BOY: We went to visit the farm. I rode on one of the farmer's trucks there!

[pause]

3

BOY: We're learning all about sheep and cows at school.
WOMAN: That's good. Do you like them?
BOY: They're OK. On Tuesday we did lots of pictures of them.
WOMAN: On Tuesday?
BOY: Yes, that's right.

[pause]

4

WOMAN: And what did you do on Saturday? You go to school that day too, I think.
BOY: Ermm ... we played football again.
WOMAN: Did you?
BOY: Oh, no. Sorry! We watched a film in the classroom that day.
WOMAN: And what was the film about?
BOY: A funny sheep that jumped on a truck and went to the city! It was OK – the farmer found it in the end.

[pause]

5

BOY: On Thursday, we had lots of work to do.
WOMAN: Reading and writing?
BOY: Yes. I read about farms on the school computer on Thursday and then I wrote a long story.
WOMAN: Great!
BOY: Yes. I know a lot about farmers and their animals now.

[pause]

Now listen to Part 3 again.

[The recording is repeated.]

That is the end of Part 3.

[pause]

Part 4　*Look at the pictures. Listen and look. There is one example.*

[pause]

What's John doing now?

[pause]

GIRL: What's John doing, Grandpa? Is he in the bath?
MAN: No, he's downstairs with Grandma. They're making Grandma's favourite – rice cakes.
GIRL: Oh! I want to go and play tennis with him!
MAN: Well, you can do that after dinner!

[pause]

Can you see the tick? Now you listen and tick the box.

[pause]

1 Which clown does Daisy like most?

GIRL: I love that clown, Dad! Look!
MAN: The one with the curly orange hair and big nose?
GIRL: They've all got big noses! No, I mean the one who's waving ... the one in the funny long shoes. He's my favourite.
MAN: Oh, I see.

[pause]

2 What did Tony dream about?

WOMAN: Good morning, Tony. Did you sleep well?
BOY: Yes, but I had a funny dream. I was on top of a big mountain, but I was in pirate's clothes!
WOMAN: Was that in the story that you read yesterday?
BOY: No, that was a story about a boy who could fly.

[pause]

3 What does Ben need?

WOMAN: I have to go to the shops today, Ben. I need a new scarf.
BOY: Oh, can you get me some new white socks, please?
WOMAN: OK. Shall I buy you a new toothbrush too?
BOY: No, I bought one yesterday.

[pause]

4 Where's Pat's favourite CD?

BOY: Mum, where's my favourite CD? It's not with my guitar.
WOMAN: Is it on the stairs, Pat? I saw it there this morning.

BOY: Well, it's not there now. Oh, here it is … under my comic!

WOMAN: Good.

[pause]

5 Which is Kim's puppy?

MAN: Right, children. Thank you for bringing all these photos of your pets to school. Kim, which one is yours?

GIRL: That puppy, Mr Last … the one with the short tail.

MAN: The brown one with big ears?

GIRL: Not that one. The one with the white face.

MAN: Oh.

[pause]

Now listen to Part 4 again.

[The recording is repeated.]

That is the end of Part 4.

[pause]

Part 5 Look at the picture. Listen and look. There is one example.

[pause]

MAN: I'd like you to do some colouring now, please.

GIRL: OK. What shall I colour first?

MAN: Can you see the rabbit?

GIRL: The rabbit? Yes, I can see that. Can I colour it brown?

MAN: Yes. Good idea!

[pause]

Can you see the brown rabbit? This is an example. Now you listen and colour and draw.

[pause]

1

MAN: Now, can you colour the road for me?

GIRL: The small road? The one with the bike on it?

MAN: That's right. Colour it yellow. Have you got that colour?

GIRL: Yes. Here it is.

[pause]

2

MAN: There are two leaves on the ground next to the bag. Can you see them?

GIRL: Yes. What colour shall I do those?

MAN: Have you got a red pencil?

GIRL: Yes.

MAN: Good. Colour the leaves on the ground with that one.

GIRL: OK!

[pause]

3

GIRL: Can I draw something in this picture, too?

MAN: Yes. How about a star? Mm, draw a star.

GIRL: Where shall I draw it?

MAN: Draw it on the boy's sweater. Can you do that?

GIRL: Yes, I can.

[pause]

4

MAN: Now … let's colour one of the clouds.

GIRL: All right. Can I do the bigger one?

MAN: Yes. Do you like blue?

GIRL: Yes, I do.

MAN: Then do the bigger cloud that colour.

GIRL: OK.

[pause]

5

GIRL: Look at the two birds.

MAN: Oh, yes! Colour one of those.

GIRL: Shall I colour the bird that's flying?

MAN: Yes, please … and colour it pink.

GIRL: All right. There …

MAN: Great! Thanks a lot.

[pause]

Now listen to Part 5 again.

[The recording is repeated.]

That is the end of the Movers Listening Test.

Reading and Writing

Part 1 (6 marks)

1 flowers   2 a monkey   3 a market
4 a jungle   5 a giraffe   6 grass

Part 2 (6 marks)

1 yes   2 yes   3 no   4 no   5 no   6 yes

Part 3 (6 marks)

1 B   2 C   3 B   4 A   5 A   6 C

Part 4 (7 marks)

1 river   2 foot   3 cry   4 box   5 afraid
6 carried   7 Two boys help some people

Part 5 (10 marks)

1 a/the/their (red) (picnic) blanket

2 mother/mum(my) and/& father/dad(dy)

3 the sea   4 Bill   5 sail   6 (green) parrot

7 an/the island   8 (the/some) coconut(s)

9 awake   10 tea

Part 6 (5 marks)

1 in   2 have   3 wash   4 some   5 which

Speaking

Part	Examiner does this:	Examiner says this:	Minimum response expected from child:	Back-up questions:
	Usher brings candidate in.	Usher to examiner: **Hello. This is (child's name)*.**		
		Examiner: **Hello, *. My name's Jane/Ms Smith.**	**Hello.**	
		How old are you, *?	*nine*	**Are you *nine/ten*?**
1	Points to **Find the differences** pictures.	**Look at these pictures. They look the same, but some things are different. This boy's playing with a robot, but this boy's playing with a truck.**		
		What other different things can you see?	Describes four other differences: • hat/no hat • one/two bags • open/closed door • white/red flowers	Point to other differences the candidate does not mention. Give first half of response: **Here the woman's wearing a hat, but here …**
2	Points to **Picture Story**. Allows time to look at the pictures.	**Now look at these pictures. They show a story. It's called 'A windy day'. Look at the pictures first.**		
		(Pause.)		
		Look at the first one.		
		Tom's sitting in a tree. He can't hold his comic because it's very windy. A girl's playing with her kite.		
		Now you tell the story. (pointing at the other pictures)	(Many variations possible) *The girl's kite is in the tree.* *She's crying.* *Tom's climbing down the tree. He's holding the kite.* *Tom's giving the kite to the girl. The woman's giving Tom his comic. They're all happy.*	Questions to prompt other parts of the story: **Where's the kite?** **What's the girl doing?** **What's Tom doing?** **What's Tom giving the girl? What's the woman giving Tom?**

* Remember to use the child's name throughout the test.

Part	Examiner does this:	Examiner says this:	Minimum response expected from child:	Back-up questions:
3	Points to **Odd-one-out** pictures.	**Now look at these four pictures. One is different. The book is different. A lemon, a pineapple and an orange are fruit. You eat them. You don't eat a book. You read it.**		
	Points to the second, third and fourth sets of pictures in turn.	**Now you tell me about these pictures. Which one is different? (Why?)**	Candidate suggests a difference (any plausible difference is acceptable).	**Where are these?** (in a bowl) **And these?** (next to the bowl) **These can all ...?** (fly) **And this animal?** (can't fly) **What are these people doing?** (phoning) **And this girl?** (singing)
4	Puts away all pictures.	**Now let's talk about you and your home.**		
		Where do you live?	*(name of town or city)*	**Do you live in *(name of town or city)*?**
		Where do you do your homework?	*living room*	**Do you do your homework in the *living room*?**
		What do you like doing at home?	*playing computer games*	**Do you like *playing computer games* at home?**
		Tell me about your house/flat.	*It's got four bedrooms.* *There's a balcony.*	**How many *bedrooms* has it got?** **Is there a *balcony*?**
		OK, thank you, *. **Goodbye.**	**Goodbye.**	

* Remember to use the child's name throughout the test.

Test 2 Answers

Listening

Part 1 (5 marks)

Lines should be drawn between:

1 Daisy and the girl under the table, with a puppy
2 Vicky and the woman with a cup and no shoes on
3 Jim and the boy with sunglasses on, with the dogs
4 Sally and the girl on the phone, with a game under her arm
5 Peter and the boy with a towel, wearing a scarf

Part 2 (5 marks)

1 Race (correct spelling)   2 lift   3 morning(s)
4 CD   5 26/twenty-six

Part 3 (5 marks)

1 Tuesday – street market, bought some red T-shirts
2 Thursday – went to the cinema and had a burger
3 Wednesday – bus ride round the city
4 Saturday – lunch in a café
5 Sunday – came home by bus

Part 4 (5 marks)

1 B   2 A   3 A   4 C   5 B

Part 5 (5 marks)

1 Colour the bag on the girl's shoulder – pink
2 Colour the socks of the standing boy – orange
3 Draw a star next to the moon on the noticeboard
4 Colour the football on the ground – yellow
5 Colour the sweater on the chair – green

TRANSCRIPT	*Hello. This is the Cambridge English Movers Listening Test.*
Part 1	*Look at Part 1. Now look at the picture. Listen and look. There is one example.*

[pause]

BOY: We had a garden party last week, Miss Long. My dad cooked sausages outside! Here's a picture!

WOMAN: Oh, yes. Is that your dad? The man in the grey shirt?

BOY: Yes. His name's Paul. Do you know him?

WOMAN: I think I do!

[pause]

Can you see the line? This is an example. Now you listen and draw lines.

[pause]

1

BOY: There's my sister, Daisy.
WOMAN: Where?
BOY: She's there, under the table with one of the puppies.
WOMAN: Oh … She looks very young!
BOY: Yes, she's only four.

[pause]

2

WOMAN: And who's that? The person with the cup in her hand?
BOY: That's one of Mum's friends.

WOMAN: What's her name?
BOY: Vicky.
WOMAN: Why hasn't she got any shoes on?
BOY: Because we've got a swimming pool in the garden. She put her feet in the water.

[pause]

3

BOY: And there's Jim. I gave him those sunglasses!
WOMAN: The boy who's sitting on the grass?
BOY: Yes. He lives in the next house. He loves our dogs.
WOMAN: I can see that!

[pause]

4

WOMAN: Who's the girl that's got the phone?
BOY: The girl with the blonde hair? That's Sally.
WOMAN: What's she carrying under her arm?
BOY: It's a new game, but we didn't play it.
WOMAN: Oh …

[pause]

5

WOMAN: What about the boy with the towel? Who's he?
BOY: That's my friend, Peter. He went in the pool too.
WOMAN: Why is he wearing a scarf?
BOY: I don't know.
Now listen to Part 1 again.

[The recording is repeated.]

That is the end of Part 1.

[pause]

Part 2 *Listen and look. There is one example.*

[pause]

GIRL: Hi, Dad.
MAN: Hello, Pat. I got an email from your school today. It was about music lessons. Would you like to learn to play the piano?
GIRL: The piano? Yes, please!
MAN: OK. I think that's a good idea too.

[pause]

Can you see the answer? Now you listen and write.

[pause]

1

GIRL: What's the piano teacher's name, Dad?
MAN: Mr Race.
GIRL: Do you spell that R-A-C-E?
MAN: That's right. Do you know Mr Race, Pat?
GIRL: No.

[pause]

2

GIRL: Where do I have to go for the lessons?
MAN: The lessons are in the room next to the lift. Let's look again. Yes, next to the lift.
GIRL: Oh, OK. I know. It's in a nice room. It's got big windows.
MAN: Has it?
GIRL: Yes.

[pause]

3

GIRL: When are the lessons? Are they on Friday afternoon? We have English then.
MAN: No. They're on Friday morning, Pat.
GIRL: Every Friday morning?
MAN: Yes, that's right. You can start next week.
GIRL: Wow! Great!

[pause]

4

GIRL: What do I have to take to the first lesson? A pen?
MAN: No, only your favourite CD. Have you got one?
GIRL: Well, I've got lots of CDs now, but I can choose a favourite one, Dad. That's easy.
MAN: Good.

[pause]

5

MAN: They said in the email please tell Pat to read page 26 of her book for her homework.
GIRL: Page 26?
MAN: Yes, that's right. Can you do that this evening?
GIRL: Can you help me?
MAN: OK!
Now listen to Part 2 again.

[The recording is repeated.]

[pause]

That is the end of Part 2.

[pause]

Part 3 *Look at the pictures. What did Jack do last week? Listen and look. There is one example.*

[pause]

WOMAN: Hello, Jack!
BOY: Oh, hello, Mrs Brown. I had a great week with my brother in the city.
WOMAN: What did you do there?
BOY: We went on a river boat on Friday. That was great! There were hundreds of ducks.
WOMAN: Oh!

[pause]

Can you see the line from the word Friday? On Friday, Jack went on a river boat. Now you listen and draw lines.

[pause]

1

WOMAN: Did you go shopping in the city?
BOY: Yes, but only to a kind of street market.
WOMAN: When did you do that?
BOY: On Tuesday … yes, that's right. We did that on Tuesday. My brother and I bought some red T-shirts.

[pause]

2

BOY: On Thursday we went to the cinema.
WOMAN: On Thursday? What did you see?
BOY: A film about a boy. His mum had a funny café. It was great.
WOMAN: Good.
BOY: Yes. Then we had a burger when we came out!

[pause]

3

BOY: We went for a ride round the city on a bus on Wednesday.
WOMAN: And did you go shopping again that day?
BOY: No. We enjoyed the ride. We sat upstairs and we could see all the city.
WOMAN: Wow! Did you take any photos?
BOY: Yes, I did.

[pause]

4

WOMAN: And what did you do on Saturday?
BOY: It rained that day but we went for a walk. And then my brother bought me some lunch in a café.
WOMAN: What did you have?
BOY: Pasta with fish and tomatoes in it. It was very good.

[pause]

5

BOY: And on Monday … sorry, Sunday, we came back home again.
WOMAN: And how did you get home?
BOY: We caught a bus from the big bus station in the city. I didn't want to go home!
WOMAN: Why?
BOY: Because the city is very exciting!
Now listen to Part 3 again.

[The recording is repeated.]

[pause]

That is the end of Part 3.

[pause]

Part 4   *Look at the pictures. Listen and look. There is one example.*

[pause]

What's the panda doing now?

[pause]

BOY: Look at this funny panda on TV, Mum!
WOMAN: What's it doing? Is it climbing that tree?
BOY: No, look, it's hiding from the tiger that's playing with the ball.
WOMAN: Oh dear!

[pause]

Can you see the tick? Now you listen and tick the box.

[pause]

1 What's in Mary's bowl?

MAN: What's in that bowl, Mary? Is it chicken?
GIRL: No, Dad. It's some vegetable soup. It's great. Would you like some?
MAN: No, thanks. I had some salad. I'm not hungry.
GIRL: OK.

[pause]

2 Where's John's book now?

BOY: Did you take my book, Mum? It's not on the table.
WOMAN: Yes, John. I put it on the stairs. Take it upstairs to your bedroom, please.
BOY: But I want to read it now.
WOMAN: Well … all right.

[pause]

3 What pet has Jane got?

GIRL: My friend Jane loves animals.
WOMAN: Does she? Has she got a kitten?
GIRL: No, she's got a rabbit. It's great!
WOMAN: When I was a girl, I had a parrot.

[pause]

4 What's Lucy's story about?

MAN: Are you reading a good story in your comic, Lucy?
GIRL: Yes, Dad.
MAN: Is it the one about the farmer?
GIRL: No, I'm reading about a clown.
MAN: Oh, I liked the one last week about the pirate.
GIRL: Oh, that one was boring.

[pause]

5 Which woman is Anna's aunt?

MAN: There's a woman in the playground with a white coat on, Anna. Do you know her?
GIRL: Yes, Mr Kite. It's my aunt.
MAN: That one who's wearing jeans?
GIRL: No. That's my cousin. My aunt's got a dress on.

Now listen to Part 4 again.

[The recording is repeated.]

[pause]

That is the end of Part 4.

[pause]

Part 5 *Look at the picture. Listen and look. There is one example.*

[pause]

GIRL: Is this a sports centre?
MAN: Yes, it is. You can see some people who are playing table tennis.
GIRL: Can I colour the glass of water on the woman's desk?
MAN: The glass of water. Yes, colour it blue.

[pause]

Can you see the blue glass? This is an example. Now you listen and colour and draw.

[pause]

1

GIRL: What can I colour now?
MAN: How about the girl's bag? The one she's carrying?
GIRL: OK. I can do that. Shall I colour that bag pink?
MAN: Yes. OK. Do you like that colour?
GIRL: Yes, I do.

[pause]

2

MAN: Now colour the boy's socks.
GIRL: The boy who's standing?
MAN: Yes, that's right.
GIRL: Can I colour his socks with my orange pencil?
MAN: Yes, you can. Good idea!
GIRL: All right. Thanks.

[pause]

3

MAN: Would you like to draw something in this picture now?
GIRL: Yes, please. What can I draw?
MAN: Can you draw a star?
GIRL: Yes, I can, but where must I draw it?
MAN: Draw the star next to the moon. The one on the board.
GIRL: OK! I'm doing that now.

[pause]

4

MAN: Can you colour one of the footballs for me now?
GIRL: Which one?
MAN: The football on the ground. Colour that one.
GIRL: Can I colour it yellow? That's my favourite colour.
MAN: Yes, OK!
GIRL: Good.

[pause]

5

GIRL: And can I colour that sweater?
MAN: The one on the armchair? OK.
GIRL: Can I do it green?
MAN: Yes, please.
GIRL: OK. I'm colouring that sweater.
MAN: Thank you. Well done!
  Now listen to Part 5 again.

[The recording is repeated.]

[pause]

That is the end of the Movers Listening Test.

Reading and Writing

Part 1 (6 marks)
1 teeth   2 ears   3 a library   4 a hospital
5 a supermarket   6 a neck

Part 2 (6 marks)
1 yes   2 no   3 no   4 yes   5 no   6 no

Part 3 (6 marks)
1 C   2 C   3 A   4 C   5 A   6 B

Part 4 (7 marks)
1 school   2 rubber   3 cage   4 windy
5 sad   6 easy   7 Monkey drawings

Part 5 (10 marks)
1 bath(time)   2 birthday / (birthday) party
3 countryside   4 a/the train   5 (big) shoes
6 (put) next to/near/by the door
7 (big/biggest/large/largest) hat   8 garden
9 closed his eyes
10 sang ((3/three/some) songs) (for him)

Part 6 (5 marks)
1 stops   2 are   3 or   4 their   5 there

Speaking

Part	Examiner does this:	Examiner says this:	Minimum response expected from child:	Back-up questions:
	Usher brings candidate in.	Usher to examiner: **Hello. This is** *(child's name)**.		
		Examiner: **Hello, *. My name's** *Jane/Ms Smith.*	Hello.	
		How old are you, *?	*nine*	**Are you** *nine/ten?*
1	Points to **Find the differences** pictures.	**Look at these pictures. They look the same, but some things are different. These are apples, but these are bananas.**		
		What other different things can you see?	Describes four other differences: • 5/2 cups	Point to other differences the candidate does not mention.
			• blue/brown bottle • boy reading comic/drawing picture • monster eating/not eating	Give first half of response: **Here there are 5 cups, but here …**
2	Points to **Picture Story.** Allows time to look at the pictures.	**These pictures show a story. It's called 'Going by boat'. Look at the pictures first. (Pause.) Look at the first one.**		
		Mary is at her grandmother's house near a river. Mary wants to go to her friend's birthday party today in the town, but there's something wrong with Grandma's car. She can't drive Mary to the party.		
		Now you tell the story. (pointing at the other pictures)	(Many variations possible) *Grandma is showing Mary an old boat.* *Grandma and Mary are going on the river in the boat.* *They are at the party.* *Mary's happy.*	Questions to prompt other parts of the story: **What's Grandma showing Mary?** **Who's in the boat?** **Where are they now?** **Is Mary happy?**

* Remember to use the child's name throughout the test.

Part	Examiner does this:	Examiner says this:	Minimum response expected from child:	Back-up questions:
3	Points to the **Odd-one-out** pictures. Points to the second, third and fourth set of pictures in turn.	**Now look at these four pictures. One is different. The book is different. A lemon, a pineapple and an orange are fruit. You eat them. You don't eat a book. You read it.** **Now you tell me about these pictures. Which one is different? (Why?)**	Candidate suggests a difference (any plausible difference is acceptable).	**These can all … ?** (fly) **And this whale?** (can't fly) **Where can you find these?** (bathroom) **And this?** (living room) **What are these people doing?** (singing) **And this boy?** (listening)
4	Puts away all pictures.	**Now let's talk about shopping.** **When do you go shopping?** **Who do you go shopping with?** **What do you like buying?** **Tell me about your favourite shop.**	 *(at) weekends* *(my) mum* *clothes* *It's very big.* *It has nice shoes.*	 **Do you go shopping *at* weekends?** **Do you go shopping with *your mum*?** **Do you like buying *clothes*?** **Is it *big* or *small*?** **What can you buy there?**
		OK, thank you, *. **Goodbye.**	 **Goodbye.**	

*Remember to use the child's name throughout the test.

Test 3 Answers

Listening

Part 1 (5 marks)

Lines should be drawn between:

1 Peter and the man with a cage of mice, wearing red jeans
2 Daisy and the woman with a dog, wearing a long skirt
3 Pat and the girl with glasses, carrying a monkey
4 Tom and the tall man, holding a snake
5 Fred and the man with a short black beard, holding a parrot

Part 2 (5 marks)

1 bus station   2 handbags   3 basement   4 cakes   5 DVDs

Part 3 (5 marks)

1 Wednesday – helped aunt in garden, went to the cinema
2 Tuesday – went to the market, bought paintings
3 Sunday – swam in the sea, saw dolphins
4 Thursday – party in garden, painted a pirate
5 Monday – went swimming in pool

Part 4 (5 marks)

1 A   2 B   3 A   4 B   5 C

Part 5 (5 marks)

1 Colour the bottle next to the bread – green
2 Write 'FOOD' on the book in the woman's hand
3 Colour the carrot between the glass and the grapes – orange
4 Colour the cheese behind the boy – yellow
5 Colour the square bowl – blue

TRANSCRIPT   *Hello. This is the Cambridge English Movers Listening Test.*

Part 1   *Look at Part 1. Now look at the picture. Listen and look. There is one example.*

[pause]

BOY: This is the new animal hospital, Grandma.
WOMAN: Oh, it's very busy in here, Jack.
BOY: Can you see that woman with the curly hair?
WOMAN: The one with the kitten?
BOY: No, the one behind the desk. That's Vicky. She's my friend's mum.
[pause]

Can you see the line? This is an example. Now you listen and draw lines.

[pause]

1

BOY: Do you see that man with the mice in the cage?
WOMAN: The man with the red jeans?
BOY: Yes, that's right.
WOMAN: What's his name?
BOY: Peter. He works with my dad.

[pause]

2

WOMAN: Can you see that woman with the dog?
BOY: The one with the long skirt?
WOMAN: Yes. Is she your mother's friend?
BOY: Yes, her name's Daisy.

[pause]

3

BOY: That girl with the glasses is my sister's friend.
WOMAN: She's carrying a monkey!

18

BOY: That's right.
WOMAN: What's her name?
BOY: Pat. She's very nice.

[pause]

4

BOY: Can you see that tall man?
WOMAN: The one who's got a snake?
BOY: Yes. It's a big snake!
WOMAN: Do you know him too?
BOY: Yes, his name's Tom. He was a teacher at my school.

[pause]

5

WOMAN: Look at that man.
BOY: The one with the black beard?
WOMAN: Yes. That's Fred. He lives in my street. Do you like his parrot?
BOY: Yes, and listen! It's talking!
WOMAN: Wow! It's very clever!

[pause]

Now listen to Part 1 again.

[The recording is repeated.]

[pause]

That is the end of Part 1.

[pause]

Part 2 *Listen and look. There is one example.*

[pause]

BOY: Can you help me with my homework, Mum?
WOMAN: Yes, Tony.
BOY: I have to write about a shop. What's your favourite one?
WOMAN: It's Golds. G-O-L-D-S.
BOY: Golds? Do you go there every week?
WOMAN: Yes, I do!

[pause]

Can you see the answer? Now you listen and write.

[pause]

1

BOY: Where is the shop?
WOMAN: It's next to the bus station.
BOY: The bus station?
WOMAN: Yes, that's right.
BOY: Oh, that's a good place for a shop.

[pause]

2

BOY: What do you buy there? Shoes?
WOMAN: You can buy lots of things there, but it's my favourite shop in town for handbags!
BOY: Handbags?
WOMAN: Yes, I bought a beautiful new one last week.

[pause]

3

WOMAN: When I go to the shop, I often have a drink.
BOY: Oh, so there's a café too.
WOMAN: Yes, it's a very big shop!
BOY: Where is the café?
WOMAN: In the basement.
BOY: Oh, I see. The basement.

[pause]

4

BOY: Can you eat pasta in the café?
WOMAN: No, they don't have hot food.
BOY: So what can you eat?
WOMAN: Well, they have great cakes.
BOY: Cakes? Oh, that's good, Mum.

[pause]

5

BOY: Can we go there on Saturday?
WOMAN: Good idea. They're giving DVDs to all the children who come to the shop this week.
BOY: That's great. I love watching DVDs!
WOMAN: Me too.

[pause]

Now listen to Part 2 again.

[The recording is repeated.]

[pause]

That is the end of Part 2.

[pause]

Part 3 *Look at the pictures. What did Jim do last week? Listen and look. There is one example.*

[pause]

WOMAN: Hello, Jim. What did you do last week on your school holiday?
BOY: Hello, Mrs White. I went to my uncle and aunt's new home. Their apartment is on a beach!
WOMAN: That's great! Did you enjoy it?
BOY: Well … on Saturday I had to help my uncle paint his boat.
WOMAN: Oh, no! Was it difficult?
BOY: Yes, but in the afternoon we went for a walk on the beach.

[pause]

Can you see the line from the word Saturday? On Saturday, Jim and his uncle painted his boat. Now you listen and draw lines.

[pause]

19

1

BOY: Wednesday was a busy day.
WOMAN: Why?
BOY: I helped my aunt in the garden. We planted some flowers.
WOMAN: Oh, did you like doing that?
BOY: It was OK. My aunt was happy because I helped her. She took me to the cinema. The film was about pirates!

[pause]

2

BOY: Friday was a nice day. Oh no, I mean Tuesday.
WOMAN: What did you do on Tuesday?
BOY: My aunt and I went to the market.
WOMAN: Did you buy something?
BOY: Yes, we bought three paintings of some boats on the sea.

[pause]

3

WOMAN: Did you go swimming in the sea?
BOY: Yes. It was exciting!
WOMAN: Which day did you do that?
BOY: Sunday. And I saw some dolphins!
WOMAN: Wow!

[pause]

4

BOY: We had a great party one day. All my uncle and aunt's friends came to see the new apartment.
WOMAN: Which day was that?
BOY: Thursday.
WOMAN: Oh, Thursday. Did you cook any nice food for them?
BOY: No, we sat in the garden. I painted a picture of a pirate.

[pause]

5

WOMAN: What did you do on Monday?
BOY: My aunt wanted to put some flowers on the balcony.
WOMAN: Did you help her?
BOY: No, not that day. I went swimming. My uncle and aunt have a swimming pool in their garden!

[pause]

Now listen to Part 3 again.

[The recording is repeated.]

[pause]

That is the end of Part 3.

[pause]

Part 4 *Look at the pictures. Listen and look. There is one example.*

[pause]

Which man is John's teacher?

[pause]

BOY: That's my teacher. Look! He's getting on the bus.
GIRL: The thin man with the blue sweater, John?
BOY: He's not wearing a blue sweater. It's grey.
GIRL: Oh, I see him. He's carrying a bag.

[pause]

Can you see the tick? Now you listen and tick the box.

[pause]

1 What must Mary take to school?

GIRL: I need to go to school now, Dad.
MAN: Have you got your baseball bat and that CD, Mary?
GIRL: No, there's no sport at school today … and the music class is on Friday.
MAN: OK.
GIRL: Oh … wait! I need my skates for the playground after school.
MAN: Please be careful!

[pause]

2 What's Alex doing upstairs?

WOMAN: Why is Alex upstairs?
BOY: He wanted to email someone but Grandma's on the computer.
WOMAN: Well, he must do his homework now.
BOY: He can't, Mum. He's texting his friend.
WOMAN: Not again!

[pause]

3 What did Ben dream about last night?

BOY: Hello, Grandpa. I had a dream last night.
MAN: Did you dream about a jungle again, Ben?
BOY: No, I was on a mountain.
MAN: Was it nice?
BOY: No. I'd like to dream about being on an island.

[pause]

4 What did Jane do at the party last night?

MAN: Was it a good party last night, Jane? Did you dance a lot?
GIRL: No. The music wasn't very good, Grandpa.
MAN: Did you eat something?
GIRL: No, I had a stomach-ache.
MAN: Oh … Did you take any photos?
GIRL: Yes, with my new camera. It was great!

[pause]

5 What was the weather like last week in Uncle Bill's village?

MAN: Look, Sam. It's raining again!
GIRL: Oh dear! The weather is never good when you come here, Uncle Bill.
MAN: Well, it was sunny last Friday. I went to sleep in the garden!
GIRL: Your village has very nice weather.
MAN: Not always. Last week it was very windy and cold!

[pause]

Now listen to Part 4 again.

[The recording is repeated.]

[pause]

That is the end of Part 4.

[pause]

Part 5   *Look at the picture. Listen and look. There is one example.*

[pause]

MAN: Look at this picture of a market!
GIRL: Can I colour something?
MAN: OK. Can you see the woman's hat?
GIRL: Yes, I can.
MAN: Colour it red.
GIRL: OK. I'm colouring her hat now.

[pause]

Can you see the red hat? This is an example. Now you listen and colour and write.

[pause]

1

GIRL: Can I colour something different now?
MAN: Yes! Would you like to colour the bottle?
GIRL: The one next to the bread?
MAN: OK. Please colour that bottle green.
GIRL: That's a nice idea!

[pause]

2

MAN: Now would you like to write something?
GIRL: Yes, what shall I write?
MAN: Write the word 'FOOD' on the big book.
GIRL: Why is the woman holding that book?
MAN: Because she wants to read about food!
GIRL: OK. I'm writing that now.

[pause]

3

GIRL: Can I do some more colouring now?
MAN: Yes. What would you like to do?
GIRL: Can I colour one of the vegetables?
MAN: OK. Please colour the carrot between the glass and the grapes. Do it orange.
GIRL: It's for the rabbit. He loves carrots.

[pause]

4

MAN: Now, can you see the cheese?
GIRL: Oh, I see it. The woman's carrying it in her shopping bag.
MAN: No, the cheese behind the boy. He dropped it!
GIRL: Can I do it yellow?
MAN: Yes, you can. Thanks!

[pause]

5

MAN: What can we do now? It's the last thing.
GIRL: I know! Can I colour the bowl?
MAN: Which one?
GIRL: The square bowl.
MAN: OK. Please do it blue.
GIRL: I like this picture a lot now!

[pause]

Now listen to Part 5 again.

[The recording is repeated.]

[pause]

That is the end of the Movers Listening Test.

Reading and Writing

Part 1 (6 marks)
1 a coat   2 a clown   3 a bear   4 a scarf
5 a doctor   6 a puppy

Part 2 (6 marks)
1 yes   2 yes   3 no   4 no   5 yes   6 no

Part 3 (6 marks)
1 B   2 B   3 A   4 A   5 B   6 C

Part 4 (7 marks)
1 shoulders   2 comic   3 milk   4 bought
5 work   6 home   7 Sally's present

Part 5 (10 marks)
1 Fish Market Square   2 5th/fifth
3 Saturday (afternoon)   4 lift/elevator
5 film/movie
6 take/get photos/photographs/pictures
7 (too) difficult   8 bedroom window
9 living room   10 waved (up)

Part 6 (5 marks)
1 than   2 at   3 their   4 drink   5 that

Speaking

Part	Examiner does this:	Examiner says this:	Minimum response expected from child:	Back-up questions:
	Usher brings candidate in.	Usher to examiner: **Hello. This is** *(child's name)**.		
		Examiner: **Hello, *. My name's** *Jane/Ms Smith.*	Hello.	
		How old are you, *?	*nine*	**Are you** *nine/ten***?**
1	Points to **Find the differences** pictures.	**Look at these pictures. They look the same, but some things are different. This ice cream is pink, but this one is green.**		
		What other different things can you see?	Describes four other differences: • glass/no glass • 3 shells/4 shells • sunny day/cloudy day • camera on towel/on sand	Point to other differences the candidate does not mention. Give first half of response: **Here the woman's holding a glass, but here ...**
2	Points to **Picture Story.** Allows time to look at the pictures.	**Now look at these pictures. They show a story. It's called 'Anna's school bag'. Just look at the pictures first. (Pause.) Look at the first one.** **Anna is on the bus. She's talking to her friend, Jane. Her school bag is on the floor.**		
		Now you tell the story. (pointing at the other pictures)	(Many variations possible) *Anna and Jane are going out of the bus, but Anna's bag is on the bus.* *A boy is picking up the bag.* *Now he's throwing the bag out of the window.* *Anna's catching the bag.*	Questions to prompt other parts of the story: **Where are the girls going?** **Where's Anna's bag?** **What's the boy doing?** **What's the boy doing now?** **What's Anna doing?**

* Remember to use the child's name throughout the test.

Part	Examiner does this:	Examiner says this:	Minimum response expected from child:	Back-up questions:
3	Points to **Odd-one-out** pictures.	**Now look at these four pictures.** **One is different. The book is different.** **A lemon, a pineapple and an orange are fruit. You eat them. You don't eat a book. You read it.**		
	Points to the second, third and fourth sets of pictures in turn.	**Now you tell me about these pictures. Which one is different? (Why?)**	Candidate suggests a difference (any plausible difference is acceptable).	**Where are these men?** (river) **And this man?** (mountains) **What are these people doing?** (sleeping) **And this girl?** (skipping) **These are all …?** (round) **And this is …?** (square)
4	Puts away all pictures.	**Now let's talk about your school.**		
		How do you go to school?	*(by) car*	**Do you go to school** *by car*?
		How many children are there in your class?	*30*	**Are there** *30* **children in your class?**
		When do you do your homework?	*(in the) evening*	**Do you do your homework** *in the evening*?
		Tell me about your English teacher.	*His/Her name's …* *He's/She's tall.*	**What's your English teacher's name?** **Is he/she** *tall*?
		OK, thank you, *. **Goodbye.**	**Goodbye.**	

* Remember to use the child's name throughout the test.

COMBINED STARTERS AND MOVERS THEMATIC VOCABULARY LIST

For ease of reference, vocabulary is arranged in semantic groups or themes. Some words appear under more than one heading.

In addition to the topics, notions and concepts listed for the syllabus, the following categories appear:

- useful words and expressions

• adjectives	• pronouns
• determiners	• verbs
• adverbs	• modals
• prepositions	• question words
• conjunctions	• names

s – first appears at *Starters*
m – first appears at *Movers*

ANIMALS

s	animal
m	bat
m	bear
s	bird
m	cage
s	cat
s	chicken
s	cow
s	crocodile
s	dog
m	dolphin
s	duck
s	elephant
s	fish (s & pl)
m	fly
s	frog
s	giraffe
s	goat
s	hippo
s	horse
m	kangaroo
m	kitten
m	lion
s	lizard
s	monkey
s	mouse/mice
m	panda
m	parrot
m	pet
m	puppy
m	rabbit
m	shark
s	sheep (s & pl)
s	snake
s	spider
s	tail
s	tiger
m	whale
s	zoo

THE BODY & FACE

s	arm
m	back
m	beard
m	blond(e)
s	body
m	curly
s	ear
s	eye
s	face
m	fair
s	foot/feet
s	hair
s	hand
s	head
s	leg
m	moustache
s	mouth
m	neck
s	nose
m	shoulder
s	smile
m	stomach
m	straight
m	tooth/teeth

CLOTHES

s	bag
s	clothes
m	coat
s	dress
s	glasses
s	handbag
s	hat
s	jacket
s	jeans
m	scarf
s	shirt
s	shoe
s	skirt
s	sock
m	sweater
s	trousers
s	T-shirt
s	watch
s	wear

COLOURS

s	black
s	blue
s	brown
s	green
s	grey (or gray)
s	orange
s	pink
s	purple
s	red
s	white
s	yellow

FAMILY & FRIENDS

m	aunt
s	baby
s	boy
s	brother
s	child/children
s	cousin
s	dad(dy)
m	daughter
s	family
s	father
s	friend
s	girl
m	granddaughter
s	grandfather
s	grandma
s	grandmother
s	grandpa

m grandparent
m grandson
m grown up
s live
s man/men
s Miss
s mother
s Mr
s Mrs
s mum(my)
s old
m parent
s person/people
s sister
m son
s their
s them
s they
m uncle
s us
s we
s woman/women
s you
s young
s your

FOOD & DRINK

s apple
s banana
s bean
m bottle
m bowl
s bread
s breakfast
s burger
s cake
s carrot
m cheese
s chicken
s chips (US fries)
s coconut
m coffee
m cup
s dinner
s drink (n & v)
s eat
s egg
s fish
s food
s fries (UK chips)
s fruit
m glass of
s grape
m hungry
s ice cream
s juice
s lemon
s lemonade
s lime
s lunch
s mango
s meat

s milk
s onion
s orange
m pasta
s pea
s pear
m picnic
s pineapple
s potato
s rice
m salad
m sandwich
s sausage
m soup
s supper
m tea
m thirsty
s tomato
m vegetable
s water
s watermelon

HEALTH

m cold
m cough
m doctor
m earache
m fine
m headache
m hospital
m hurt
m matter (What's the matter?)
m nurse
m stomach-ache
m temperature
m toothache

THE HOME

m address
s apartment
s armchair
m balcony
m basement
s bath
s bathroom
s bed
s bedroom
m blanket
s bookcase
s box
s camera
s chair
s clock
s computer
s cupboard
s desk
s dining room
s doll
s door
m downstairs
m dream
m elevator

m fan
s flat
s floor
s flower
s garden
s hall
m home
s house
s kitchen
s lamp
m lift
s living room
s mat
s mirror
s painting
s phone
s picture
s radio
s room
m shopping
m shower
s sleep
s sofa
m stair(s)
s table
s television/TV
m toothbrush
m towel
s toy
s tree
m upstairs
s wall
m wash (n & v)
s watch
s window

NUMBERS

s Cardinals: 1–20
m Cardinals: 21–100
m Ordinals: 1st–20th

PLACES & DIRECTIONS

m above
m bank
s behind
s between
m bus station
m café
m cinema
m farm
s here
m hospital
s in
s in front of
m library
m map
m market
s next to
s on
s park
m place
m playground

m road
s shop (US store)
m square
s store (UK shop)
m straight
s street
m supermarket
m swimming pool
s there
s under
s zoo

SCHOOL

s alphabet
s answer
s ask
s board
s book
s bookcase
s class
s classroom
s close
s colour
s computer
s correct
s cross
s cupboard
s desk
s door
s draw(ing)
s English
s eraser
s example
s find
s floor
m homework
s know
s learn
s lesson
s letter (as in alphabet)
s line
s listen (to)
s look
m mistake
s name
s number
s open
s page
s part
s pen
s pencil
s picture
s playground
s question
s read
s right (as in correct)
s rubber
s ruler
s school
s sentence
s spell
s stand (up)

s story
s teacher
s tell
s test (n & v)
m text
s tick (n & v)
s understand
s wall
s window
s word
s write

SPORTS & LEISURE

s badminton
s ball
s baseball
s basketball
m bat
s beach
s bike
s boat
s book
s bounce
s camera
s catch
m CD
m comic/comic book
s doll
s draw(ing)
s drive (v)
m DVD
s enjoy
s favourite
m film
s fish(ing)
s fly
s football (US soccer)
s game
s guitar
s hit
s hobby
s hockey
m holiday
s jump
s kick (v)
m kick (n)
s kite
s listen (to)
m movie
m music
s paint(ing)
m party
s photo
s piano
s picture
s play (with)
m present
s radio
s read
s ride (n & v)
s run
m sail

s sing
m skate
s soccer (UK football)
s song
s sport
m sports centre
s story
m swim (n)
m swimming pool
s table tennis
s television/TV
s tennis
s throw
m towel
s toy
s TV/television
m video
m walk (n)
s watch

TIME

m after
s afternoon
m age
m always
m before
s birthday
s clock
s day
s end
s evening
m every
s morning
m never
s night
m sometimes
s today
s watch
m week
m weekend
m yesterday
The days of the week:
m Sunday
m Monday
m Tuesday
m Wednesday
m Thursday
m Friday
m Saturday

TOYS

s ball
s baseball
s basketball
s bike
s car
s doll
s football
s game
s helicopter
s kite
s lorry (US truck)

s monster
s plane
s robot
s toy
s train
m treasure
s truck (UK lorry)

TRANSPORT

s bike
s boat
s bus
m bus station
s car
m drive
m driver
s fly
s go
s helicopter
s lorry (US truck)
s motorbike
s plane
m ride (n)
s ride (v)
s run
s swim
m ticket
s train
s truck (UK lorry)
s walk

WEATHER

m cloud
m cloudy
m rain
m rainbow
m snow
s sun
m sunny
m weather
m wind
m windy

WORK

m clown
m doctor
m farmer
m hospital
m nurse
m pirate
s teacher
m work

THE WORLD AROUND US

s beach
m city
m country(side)
m field
m forest
m grass
m ground

m island
m jungle
m lake
m leaf/leaves
m moon
m mountain
m plant
m river
m road
m rock
s sand
s sea
s shell
m star
s street
s sun
m town
s tree
m village
s water
m waterfall
m world

USEFUL WORDS & EXPRESSIONS

s bye (-bye)
m come on!
m excuse me
s goodbye
s hello
s I don't know
s no
s oh
s oh dear
s OK
s pardon
s please
s right
m see you!
s so
s sorry
s thank you
s thanks
s then
s well
s well done
s wow
s yes

ADJECTIVES

m afraid
m all
m all right
s angry
m awake
m back
m bad
s beautiful
m best
m better
s big
m boring

m bottom
m busy
m careful
s clean
m clever
s closed
m cloudy
m cold
s correct
m different
m difficult
s dirty
s double
m easy
s English
m every
m exciting
m famous
m fat
s favourite
m fine
m first
s funny
s good
s great
s happy
s her
s his
m hot
m hungry
s its
m last
s long
m loud
m more
m most
s my
m naughty
s new
s nice
s old
s our
m quick
m quiet
s right (correct)
m round
s sad
m second
s short
m slow
s small
s sorry
m square
m straight
m strong
m surprised
m tall
m terrible
s their
m thin
m third
m thirsty
m tired

m top
s ugly
m weak
m well
m wet
m windy
m worse
m worst
m wrong
s young
s your

DETERMINERS

s a/an
s a lot of
m all
m another
m any
m both
m every
s lots of
s many
m more
m most
s my
s no
s one
s some
s that
s the
s these
s this
s those

ADVERBS

s a lot
s again
m all right
m always
m back
m badly
m best
m better
m carefully
m down
m downstairs
m first
s here
m how
m how much
m how often
m inside
m last
s lots
m loudly
m more
m most
m near
m never
s not
s now
m off
m often

m on
m only
m out
m outside
m quickly
m quietly
m round
m slowly
m sometimes
s then
s there
s today
s too
m up
m upstairs
s very
m well
m when
m worse
m worst
m yesterday

PREPOSITIONS

s about
m above
m after
s at
m before
s behind
m below
s between
m by
m down
s for
s from
s in (prep of place)
m in (prep of time)
s in front of
m inside
s like
m near
s next to
s of
m off
s on (prep of place)
m on (prep of time)
m opposite
m out of
m outside
m round
m than
s to
s under
m up
s with

CONJUNCTIONS

s and
m because
s but
s or
m than
m when

PRONOUNS

m all
m another
m both
s he
s her
s hers
s him
s his
s I
s it
s its
s me
s mine
m more
m most
m nothing
s one
s ours
s she
m something
s that
s theirs
s them
s these
s they
s this
s those
s us
s we
m which
m who
s you
s yours

VERBS

Irregular:
s be
m bring
m buy
s catch (a ball)
m catch (a bus)
s choose
s come
s do
s draw
s drink
s drive
s eat
s find
s fly
s get
m get (un)dressed
m get up
s give
s go
m go shopping
s have
s have (got)
m have (got) to
m hide
s hit
s hold

m hurt
s know
s learn
m lose
s make
m mean
m must
s put
m put on
s read
s ride
s run
s say
s see
s sing
s sit (down)
s sleep
s spell
s stand (up)
s swim
m take
m take (a bus)
s take (a photo)
m take off
s tell
m think
s throw
s understand
m wake up
s wear
s write

Regular:
s add
s answer
s ask
s bounce
m call
m carry
s clean
m climb
s close
s colour
s complete
m cook
s cross
m cry
m dance
m dream
m drop
m email
s enjoy
m film
m fish
m help
m hop
m invite
s jump
s kick
m laugh
s learn
s like
s listen (to)

s live
s look
s look at
m look for
s love
m move
m need
s open
s paint
s phone
s pick up
m plant
s play (with)
s point
m rain
m sail
m shop
m shout
s show
m skate
m skip
s smile
m snow
s start
s stop
s talk
s test
m text
s tick
s try
m video
m wait
s walk
s want
m wash
s watch
s wave
m work

MODALS

s can/cannot/can't
m could
m must
m shall
m would

QUESTION WORDS

s how
s how many
m how much
m how often
s how old
s what
m when
s where
s which
s who
s whose
m why

NAMES

s Alex
s Ann
s Anna
s Ben
s Bill
m Charlie
m Daisy
s Dan
m Fred
s Grace
m Jack
m Jane
s Jill
m Jim
m John
s Kim
m Lily
s Lucy
m Mary
s May
s Nick
s Pat
m Paul
m Peter
m Sally
s Sam
s Sue
s Tom
s Tony
m Vicky